MW01029237

The Windows of Faith

Prayers of Holy Hildegard

Hildegard of Bingen

Edited by Walburga Storch, O.S.B.
Translated by Linda M. Maloney
Introduction by Caecilia Bonn, O.S.B.

A Liturgical Press Book

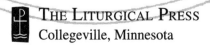

THE LITURGICAL PRESS
Collegeville, Minnesota

Cover design by Greg Becker

A translation of *Gebete der Heiligen Hildegard. An den Fenstern des Glaubens,* published by Pattloch Verlag, Augsburg, 1991.

© 1997 by The Order of St. Benedict, Inc., Collegeville, Minnesota. All rights reserved. No part of this book may be reproduced in any form or by any means, electronic or mechanical, including photocopying, recording, taping, or any retrieval system, without the written permission of The Liturgical Press, Collegeville, Minnesota 56321. Printed in the United States of America.

1	2	3	4	5	6	7	8

Library of Congress Cataloging-in-Publication Data
Hildegard, Saint, 1098–1179.
   [Selections. English. 1997]
   The windows of faith : prayers of Holy Hildegard / Hildegard of Bingen.
     p. cm.
   Translation of: Gebete der Heilegen Hildegard. Augsburg : Pattloch Verlag, 1991.
   ISBN 0-8146-2448-0
   1. Prayers, Medieval. I. Title.
BV237.H44213   1997
242'.802—dc21   97-13970
                                         CIP

Contents

Foreword

I was happy to respond to Pattloch Verlag's request to collect the prayers of Saint Hildegard because these texts, scattered throughout her major theological works, are especially appealing to us today. In their honesty and simplicity they reveal the heart of the saint and reflect the inner stages through which a human being passes on its pilgrimage from God to God.

Each of us has a history, and our lives are a constant movement of ascent and descent through light and darkness, joy and suffering. I have attempted to give expression to this movement through a corresponding sequence of prayers, and I have given each prayer a title indicating its theme.

"Bis orat qui cantat": to sing is to pray twice, as St. Augustine said. Prior Caecilia Bonn suggested that I include some of Hildegard's challenging song texts in this little book. Sister Caecilia has studied the work of our great patroness longer than I, and I am grateful to her for her helpful suggestions and support in giving verbal shape to these "sung prayers." I hope that her introduction to this prayerbook will lure many people toward the "windows of faith," and may the "Teutonic prophet" prove herself a powerful advocate for her homeland.

Walburga Storch, O.S.B.
Benedictine Abbey of St. Hildegard,
Rüdesheim/Eibingen
Feast of the Epiphany, 1991

Introduction to Hildegard's Thought World

> "How can I project thoughts on someone who passes me in silence?"
>
> —Hildegard of Bingen

In the heart's conversation with God human beings reveal their personalities at the deepest and most profoundly authentic level. Here they are entirely themselves and express who they really are. That is why we return again and again to the prayers of the saints, where they show their true faces, where we encounter their personalities at their central core. The prayers of the saints can also be a help to the often tongue-tied people of our age. They give us courage to overcome the speechlessness of our own hearts, so often and so painfully experienced, and they can show us where we stand on the way to the goal of our pilgrimage.

Hildegard of Bingen (1098–1179) did not leave us a prayer-book in the classic sense, nothing we could call the "history of a soul." In that regard she is different from the great women of the Cistercian order, for example Saint Gertrude the Great or the two Mechtilds of Magdeburg and Hackeborn, who lived just a half century later and represent the high point of medieval mysticism: a new intensity of the German spirit, an expression of bridal ardor and the fiery glow of the divine presence.

Hildegard, who often spoke of herself as "God's trumpet," was first and primarily a prophet, and she herself felt that calling to be a heavy burden. The God revealed to her did not show her the divine presence in order to draw her God-ward in mystical union, but in order to approach a human listener. Thus while every one of her visions begins with the very personal "I," that "I" is like a door through which another enters, and that other is God. Hildegard was made a servant of the proclamation of salvation that from the deepest beginnings of the divine plan has been directed to and encompasses the whole human race.

Dialogue between God and the Human

Hildegard's mystical writings from which the prayers, songs, and texts of this collection are drawn are not meant to present an exclusive dialogue between God and the soul. Instead they address a human person whose physical nature unites her inextricably with the whole of creation and who thereby becomes the epitome of all created things. In this key position between the vertical and the horizontal the human being not only has the task of responding within the conversation God has initiated but is responsible for extending it to all creatures. If human beings truly desire to realize their humanity they must, according to the "prophet of the Rhineland," throw themselves into the current of this comprehensive conversation. "Come, let us talk with one another"—that is, we are invited to pray. Prayer thus becomes a dialogue on all levels: dialogue between the Creator and the creature, between human beings, between the human and nature, between the individual and history, between body and soul, between vices and virtues.

The matter of this conversation, inexhaustible and always new, is love. The dialogue between God and the human person arises out of the mutual love of Creator and creature. "Thus all the creature's obedience is only a desire for the kiss of the Creator who gives to the world everything it needs."

God is self-revealed as "through a window" to the person who looks to God in faith. We need this gaze upward and outward into transcendence if we hope to understand the symbols of creation and of our own being and interpret them rightly. For Hildegard, to have faith means not separating the earthly from the heavenly, for "every creature has a visible and an invisible component. The visible is weak, the invisible strong and vital." Every bit of the this-worldly has its counterpart in a piece of the other-worldly. Faith demolishes the wall of a world closed and locked within itself and opens a window into the divine realm. Therefore to pray means to stand at the window of faith, to see, to hear, to respond and be responsible.

The first part of the prayers of Hildegard here presented contains texts that were not conceived or composed as prayers, but are taken from the flow of her visions. It is true that for that very reason they place no small demands on the reader, for the larger context from which they are taken is not always evident and God, the dialogue partner, does not speak. Nevertheless we hope that they will be especially helpful to people of today who so often find themselves speechless toward God, because they present not a shred of "pious prattle" and expose the bedrock of the human heart.

Wonder, Praise, and Adoration

In the second part of the collection the editor has selected twenty-six poems from the seventy-six spiritual songs of the prophet of the Rhineland. They are essentially different from the previous prayers because the texts and musical settings were carefully and artistically composed by Hildegard and adapted for liturgical use. Those who know the stormy, dynamic, and emotional music of these songs will sense the Gothic stylistic mood that governs them. The texts themselves were born out of the fire of her visions and can scarcely be bound by meter and rhythm. They are the expressions of wonder, praise, and adoration. Within them the visions are concentrated and the experience of the "intimate knower of God" with God and the world is crystallized.

In order to give the readers of this book some help for deciphering and achieving a deeper understanding of Hildegard's prayer language, let me address a few focal points of her spirituality.

The Mystery of the Beginning. In the works of this saint there is scarcely a hint of the mysticism of the heart of Jesus and his passion, a mystical movement then in its earliest stages. Hildegard's gaze was turned to the heart of the Father and Creator who appeared to her "shiningly enthroned." The "Father's utter kindness" is the focal point of all the dramatic events involving God, the human being, and the world. That is the true home of every human person. Like a tiny, heart-shaped, soiled lump of clay, it rests in the heart of the Father who lovingly cleanses it, cares for it, and adorns it. Out of the heart of our creator we are embraced, kissed, and placed in existence. From this "mystery of the beginning" comes the "fundamental desire for the embrace and kiss, without which we would wither away" that exists in every human being. At the bottom of our hearts, therefore, we can never be rid of the memory of our origin, which is also our end, for God, in the infinity of divine kindness, by creating us becomes our mother. Christ in becoming human became our brother because he received life-giving nourishment from the same source, the "motherly breast" (of the Father).

Therefore nothing is "sweeter" to a human being than to run toward the creator of the universe. "I will follow you because you are my creator." The creature knows that it has grown from and is touched by its creator. Creatures are, in turn, entitled to see, know, touch, and enjoy their God and to rest in the divine embrace. Thus those who pray in the words of Saint Hildegard are conscious of their dignity as creatures. While they can produce nothing good of themselves, by turning to God in prayer they have the entire creative power of their Lord placed at their disposal. Hildegard sees something that is reserved for the vision of the angels who see God face to face: how the heart of the Father breathes forth its innermost power, a divine dynamic *(virtutes)* that builds up, heals, and averts everything that is chaotic and deadly. In the human being this power becomes virtue and empowers her or him for work in the world. Thus the human being becomes a coworker of God, and in a certain sense a creator: in calling out to the creator in prayer the creature comes to itself and finds itself equipped for its task. Hildegard seems almost to be giving a definition of the human person when she writes: "The created human being is like a call, a cry, a voice. O how pitiful and at the same time wonderful is this voice, because God has adorned these fragile vessels with all the divine wonders under heaven."

The Brokenness of the Human. Face to face with their God, however, human beings not only recognize their dignity but at the same time acknowledge with deep shock the depthless mis-

ery of their brokenness, for they "have forgotten their creator."
Hildegard avows: "Like ashes and the filth of ashes do I appear
to myself in the depth of my soul, and like dust that blows away.
I am not worthy to be called human. Great is my fear." And even
when she was very old she begged her secretary, Wilbert of
Gembloux, "Pray that I may not fall, for even Peter could not
stand fast."

Like a stranger driven from his inheritance, homeless and
bereft of all joy—in prison and in chains—that is how the sinful
human being experiences himself, for he has not only sinned
against his Lord but at the same time alienated God's creation in
his own existence and thereby extinguished his own face. This
misery of sinful existence appears again and again in a great vari-
ety of images in Hildegard's prayers; it is rooted in forgetfulness
of God and a bitter silence. "I behold my wounds." The dignity
and misery of the human being: how can we live without be-
traying the one to the other or being constantly dragged back-
ward and forward, sinners and justified as well? How can we take
charge of the artistic work of our Christian life and join the two
together? In face of this question Hildegard introduces the
strongest and most beautiful tones of her spirituality in speaking
of the all-powerful might of repentance. Her works are deeply
imbued with the image of the prodigal son returning to the father.
Because the themes of repentance and sighing play a great role in
her prayers as well we must speak of them at greater length.

The Creative Power of Repentance. "The shining one on the
mountain" is, for Hildegard, constantly at work transforming the
miry clay, the suppurating wounds, and the broken limbs of the
sinner into pearls and precious gems by immersing them in the
light of the infinite divine goodness. This is done in the power of
the blood of the Son who desires to return those who have gone
astray to the Father through his own wounds. But this cannot be
accomplished without human effort. Hildegard says that heaven
and earth are shaken when a human being pauses on her false
course, remembers her creator, looks up to God and begins to
speak: "I will arise and return to my Father." Thus conversion
begins when a human being becomes aware of her wounds and
ceases to hide and deny them. "I seek the wounds of your heart,"
says the Human One, "show me the wounds of your heart."

11

When we show him our wounds, the Son of God responds by showing us his own. "I will suffer with you in your wounds and so I will give you communion with the Father."

At this moment, by the touch of grace, the sinner makes the crucial step. He turns from himself, awakes as if from sleep, rises eagerly, impelled by the driving force of repentance, and hastens back to the Father. "Therefore I will immediately and unconditionally receive him and deliver him to freedom." In the embrace of God, in the mystery of their origins, human beings come to themselves, escape the slavery of sin, and are made whole, not because they have struggled with their own shadows or healed themselves, but because they have run to God. For Hildegard this step toward God is the most important moment of the spiritual life. "I will be with those who comprehend me through true penance. In them I will even wed myself to human filth, because I will purify it."

Thus repentance, for Hildegard, is the true medicine not only for the soul, but for the body as well. Without it all the healing arts can only combat symptoms. Far from loading human beings down with feelings of guilt, repentance instead frees them from the rule of fear. But repentance not only has healing power; on it rest the pillars of the universe: its power moves and alters the life processes of history and the cosmos. With it "we touch the stars." Through it God brings home the creation that human beings have poisoned.

Sighing for God. In this connection we need to reflect on still another word whose meaning has probably faded for us altogether; nevertheless, it played an important role for Hildegard. It is the spiritual "sigh." Thinking of God and our true home in God and at the same time remembering our wounds gives rise to a penetrating twofold pain: longing for God and the experience of one's own powerlessness. This torturing pain expresses itself in a sigh and tears human beings away from themselves and toward God. It is thus an important event occurring within both body and soul that counters every kind of repression. "Body and soul make a covenant and express themselves together in a sigh. That is heaven: to lift myself up in the true sighing of desire. In my deep sighing I behold God." No one can "fashion" a sigh, but one can make oneself available for it.

12

The eighth chapter of Paul's letter to the Romans gives us a theology of sighing. Paul describes how all nature sighs and groans in labor pains. So also human beings sigh and groan in awaiting their redemption. But since we do not know how we ought to pray the Spirit prays on our behalf with unutterable sighs, crying out to the Father (Rom 8:22-26). Therefore it is Godself in us who drives us to sighing. Hence Hildegard can say categorically, "whoever lacks the Spirit's sighing will not believe." That is, such people will not surrender totally, will not allow God to enter into their flesh. In sighing we touch the heart of God, like a child that, after a hard and painful experience, throws itself into its father's or mother's lap and clings to them.

Hildegard disputes the possible objection "but if I cannot sigh, that's just the way it is" by saying: "You are forbidding your soul to weep and sigh and preventing it from seeking help in me. But how can I answer someone whose voice I do not hear? You do not sigh to me any more, and thus you ask nothing of me. Whoever does not sigh for me with longing has forgotten me."

The Works of Virtue. For Hildegard repentance already constitutes the first of the so-called good works. Whenever a person comes to one of life's crossroads and makes the free decision, each time, to take the homeward road to the creator, he or she follows the way of God's commandments "as the deer hastens to the spring." For such a person the commandments are not legal prescriptions or ascetic imperatives; she or he finds joy in them, can even "savor" them. In doing good deeds, the works of virtue, a person becomes a coworker with God. The strength for these works comes from the heart of the creator as a bride comes to the bridegroom, and invites the person to loving union whose fruit is the works of virtue. In doing them one glorifies God, comes to oneself, and is able to build up this world and the world to come. Decisiveness is therefore demanded: a person is an existence at the parting of the ways between good and evil. If one fails in the good there is only one alternative: the way of repentance. Everything else belongs to the realm of death.

It is possible that some of Saint Hildegard's expressions when she speaks of this topic could give the impression of hatred of the body, since for her the decision for the good constitutes a continual struggle against the desires and lusts of the flesh. But with the word "flesh" Hildegard speaks, very much in the biblical sense, of the evil and God-avoiding tendency of fallen human nature. Against this she clearly sets up a positive spirituality of bodiliness that was revolutionary for her time. "As is worthy of the creator, you clothed me with pure flesh . . . spread out the hem of your garment and girded me with the belt of your praise. . . . The soul can do nothing without the body; it needs it in order to express itself fittingly; indeed, the soul takes pleasure in working within the body." Soul and body are thus not rivals struggling against one another; they are born to be partners. Their cooperation is, of course, not without conflicts but for that very reason the two must remain in conversation with one another and care for each other like lovers in order to carry out their work for God. "The aroma of good works streams forth from the body," for a human being is always and entirely embodiedness.

In the House of Glory

The twenty-six songs included in the second part of this collection are undoubtedly some of the "thickest" of Hildegard's texts. In them all she has said and prayed culminates in marvel, praise, and adoration. In the golden city beyond the window she sees the completed edifice of the infinite goodness of the Father for which believers in this life are to collect and prepare the stones. The golden city, the house of the glory of her Lord becomes her home, and she cries out to Zion her mother. She longs for the sound of the perfected harmony of all things in communion with the choir of angels.

That is why her spiritual songs so often exclaim "O." That is also the reason for the wide-leaping intervals in the notation that shatter the sober discipline and contemplative calm of classic Gregorian choral music. Nevertheless, here again out of the dense fullness of the content flows the clear objectivity of her gaze.

Mary, the Primal Image of Creation and the Church

At the nodal point of heaven and earth, God and the human, Hildegard in her songs again and again encounters Mary, whom

14

the Church's liturgy eulogizes as the "gate of heaven." The eleven poems to her presented here are among the most precious pearls of Marian hymnody. Eyewitnesses reported, in the canonization documents of Saint Hildegard, that love for Mary surrounded her like a halo when she sang with her sisters in the monastic choir.

These songs are enlivened by a multitude of images that we should simply allow to wash over us. Still, a few guidelines may help us to rediscover Mary in these songs today.

Hildegard is here both poet and theologian. For her the figure of the mother of the Lord displays cosmic features above all. The creator of the world "before all creatures beholds the countenance of the most beautiful of all women, as the eagle looks into the sun." This is a bold image. As in a mirror the creator beholds in Mary the unspoiled and uncorrupted concept of the great divine plan. So she becomes the "embrace of all creation." Therefore Hildegard interprets the wisdom texts of the Old Testament as referring to Mary:

> The Lord created me at the beginning of his work, the first of his acts of long ago. Ages ago I was set up, at the first, before the beginning of the earth. When there were no depths I was brought forth, when there were no springs abounding with water. . . . When he established the heavens, I was there, . . . when he made firm the skies above, . . . I was his daily delight, rejoicing before him always . . . (Prov 8:22-30).

Mary is the dawn, the glowing original matter, the golden foundation of the world as it is filled and penetrated by God. As the second Eve she is the helper from and at the side of the Son of God. She becomes the mother of the living and the original source of life. Certainly Hildegard clearly distances herself from every kind of sentimental or archaic cult of a primal mother. She describes Mary's uniqueness as the unspoiled existence of model virginity, having nothing to do with ascetic achievement but totally and in its entirety an existence in grace. "Your chastity is glory from God, perfect creation."

The gaze of the poet and singer returns again and again to the body, the fruitful womb of the virgin. The unutterable mystery, the mighty event of the incarnation draws her under its spell. On the very first day of creation God entrusted to the womb of Mary not only the only-begotten, eternal divine Son, but also God's work of salvation, the Church. There Mary gathers "the members of the lovely body of her son" to a unity. Therefore in the womb of the virgin begin, for Hildegard, the first tones of the perfect symphony of heaven.

But Mary is not only the shining, golden original material of creation, she is also the ultimate womb of all sanctity, the constructive force of life, the life-giving instrument. She reflects the way in which grace perfects nature. The mystery of the Church is thus unveiled in a series of images. Mary and the Church are bound together and mutually revelatory. Mary is the Church in person. The images remain open in both directions. Zion as mother can be either the Church or Mary, and ultimately the motherly love of God.

As the one who is utterly and completely whole Mary is also the mother of the healing arts; in fact she herself is the soothing balm for the wounds of our brokenness after Eve's fall. Yet she shows her motherly compassion for us in other ways. As the one always and completely filled by the Holy Spirit she stands as a prophet on our path and calls to us again and again, with loud cries, to come out of our ruined state. In the power of the Holy Spirit who continually overshadows Mary and makes her fruitful she becomes the woman who saves the whole human race. The Holy Spirit is for her the "dynamo of the universe and root of creation."

The Holy Spirit as Life-Force

Who is the Holy Spirit of God? In two of her songs Hildegard gives us an answer to this question. She calls the Spirit the Living One, the most intimate impulse and moving force of every life. The Spirit is the "life of life." For Hildegard life has a comprehensive meaning. Concretely and first of all it is creation. "Through you the clouds waft and the breezes blow, stones drip and brooks burst forth from their springs, making green things sprout from the earth." All creation in every one of its processes has to do with the life-giving Spirit of God. Wherever we encounter life we can experience the Spirit's power and we are moved by God. "Life of the life of all created things, . . . you give life to every form."

But life is also wisdom and understanding. King Solomon preferred the gift of wisdom to all riches and every kind of power. "You continually produce people full of understanding, made glad by the breath of wisdom." In wisdom and understanding the human being is open and able to receive life-creating power from the heart of God in order to make use of it in the world. The Holy Spirit impels us to act, breathes within all our actions, and thus is available for our enjoyment. "Sweetness" is what the spiritual teacher and mystic calls the unutterable that we experience when the breath of God touches us and invites us to love. The Spirit of God is holy. Through the Spirit "the universe glows and catches fire." The Spirit drives and moves human beings to good works through the "fiery power" that is proper to the Spirit, by means of which human persons are able to build and to heal, through which the Spirit can overcome everything that sets itself against life. The Holy Spirit is a pure source of water and a mirror in which we can see how God deals with sinners and their brokenness. "You anoint those who are dangerously wounded, you cleanse suppurating wounds." Here Hildegard is again engaged with her favorite topic, repentance. "You built another tower out of toll collectors and sinners, so that they would confess their sins and deeds before you. Therefore all creatures praise you . . . for you are the most precious ointment for broken limbs and festering wounds, which you transform into precious pearls."

Here the holiness of the Spirit of God is sung in the mystery of inexhaustible mercy. Truly, the "power of God will save you." The plan of salvation, however, is at the same time a plan of union: "You hope of the members for unity." For modern people, in contrast, a great deal has come apart. They themselves have been cut loose from the web of relationships and have succeeded in separating everything from all else. But God's Spirit desires to gather and bind into unity. "You powerful way that traverses all things . . . you ordain and encompass all in one." The Holy Spirit is the guarantor of human dignity and the joy of life. The Spirit is the sound and the voice of our praise.

Perfection in Christ

All our prayers originate and have their goal in the dialogue of the Son of God with the Father. There, before all time, flows the uninterrupted conversation into which we are invited. Our impoverished and timid address to heaven is sustained by it, is surrounded by it, and flows into it. Thus it is right that this collection should close with the moving word of the Son to the Father that Hildegard placed at the conclusion and climax of her major work "World and Humanity," and her little drama "Powers at Play." Imploringly the Son shows the Father his wounds, which remain open as long as any human being on earth still sins. Christ shows his stigmata not only as a sign of his incarnation but as the deepest expression of his solidarity with us sinners, and with the entire withering and fading creation.

> In the beginning all creation was greening . . . but then the power of life dried up. Remember, O Father! The hopes of the beginning should not have withered. . . . Father, look, I am your Son! . . . Behold the wounds . . . have mercy . . . ! Through the blood of my wounds bring them in penitence back to you.

The great themes of Hildegard's visions are touched upon once more in this last prayer: the fall and restoration of creation, the healing of sinful human beings by the showing of their wounds and redemptive union with the wounds of the Lord. The prayer closes with the prophetic call to kneel in adoration before the creator and Father that he may reach out his hand to heal so that his beloved work may be perfected in human beings.

The readers of this book are invited to surrender with their whole hearts to these words of the prayers of Saint Hildegard. In them one of the greatest Christian women left us, almost nine hundred years ago, a moving testimony of living faith. This little book will have accomplished its purpose if even one text can open a conversation with God in the heart of the one who reads it and bring it about—God grant it!—that the reader may utter a single sigh.

Sister Caecilia Bonn, O.S.B.

Prayers

Painful Pilgrimage

I wander aimlessly in the shadow of death
as a pilgrim in a strange land;
my consolation is the goal of my wandering.

I was to have been a companion of the angels,
your living breath, O God, in a vessel of clay.
Should I not recognize and feel you?

Alas, my tent has turned
the body's eye to the north!
There I was imprisoned and—oh!—
robbed of light and the joy of knowledge,
my whole garment was torn!
I have been driven from my heritage
and led away into slavery.

Where am I? How came I here?
Who will comfort me in prison?
How can I rend these chains?
Who will care for my wounds,
anoint them with oil and have pity?

O heaven, hear my cry,
let the earth tremble with me for sorrow!
I am a stranger far from comfort,
far from aid.

Abandonment

Who will console me since my mother
has left me far distant from the way of salvation?
O Mother Sion, see, I remember
joy in the house of your glory.
Where shall I flee?
My pain is unspeakable;
Where are you, O Mother Sion?

For a brief moment I sensed your presence
and hoped I might return home;
will you abandon me again?
I, most miserable, turned from you . . .
Oh, had I never known you
my pain would be easier to bear.
With tears and sighs I call to you:
where is your help for me?

Doubt

O God, are you not my maker?
The suffering earth oppresses me!
I have to take flight like Adam,
hide myself from your face.
My sinful life tries to ignore you;
I despair of understanding righteousness;
the struggle robs me of all my joy.
Do I know whether God exists?
Where is my king and my God?

Repentance

I will turn to the East
and begin to follow the narrow path.
You alone, O God, can help me!
Without you I can do no good thing.
To you I look up;
you give me life.
Oh, let me know your kindness!

To you, blessed Virgin, I will hasten,
 to grasp the strong shield of your humility
and join my voice to the choir of angels:
Praise to you, O God!

God's Help

My God, it is you who made me,
I live through you and seek after you
when, sighing, I implore what is good.

Of course I acknowledge you are my God
and know only that I may serve you
because you have given me understanding.

O my helper in all that is good,
through you I accomplish my good works.
On you I cast all my hope
and I put on your protection like a cloak.

You are my savior: preserve me from evil
when my conscience warns me
to abandon what is evil.

The Way to the Light

O God, you have given me two eyes
to see in the darkness a glorious light,
to choose the way I ought to go.
Now whether I see or am blind
I know that I need someone to lead me
toward the day and also to the night.

For when I hide myself in darkness
I can act very boldly;
but in the light I am visible
and instead of reward, I bring punishment on myself
for doing the selfsame thing.

Living God, I cry to you,
lead me on the way of light
and heal my dreadful sores
so that I need not be ashamed in the light of day.
Sever the shackles of my imprisonment!

Repentance and Return

Father, I have sinned
against heaven and against myself,
the heavenly work that I am.
Fashioned by you, touched by you,
I should have done heavenly things.
But because I have destroyed my human nature
I have also sinned before you.

My ruin is my own fault.
I am no longer worthy
to be called your child
because I have alienated your creation in myself,
turned it of my own accord
away from the purpose for which you made it.

Now treat me as your servant
whom you have so dearly bought back
in the blood of your Son!

In Adam I lost the inheritance of the children,
but now repentance will buy my freedom
from all my sins
with the blood of your Son.

The Work of God

I will rejoice, O my God,
because you shelter and defend me;
you free me from the burden of sin.
Now my soul longs to follow you
with its good works.
I was called by you out of deep groaning,
drawn by your power;
you have made a safe place for me with you,
saved me from my enemies.

I am indeed the work that you made;
you determined before all time
that you would form me as I am
and place all creation at my feet.
You then made me able
to make my works like yours,
and so I belong to you alone.

As is worthy of the creator
you clothed me with pure flesh,
spread out the hem of your garment
and girded me with the belt of your praise.
Whoever sees you with the eyes of faith,
 three-personed God, will never be destroyed.

Inconstancy

O all-knowing God who made all good,
I shudder as I acknowledge my sin.
I do repent and recognize myself,
but my repentance is ineffective
and fear abides in me.

On the paths of self-will
fear seizes me despite my pride;
I grow old in my sins.
Although they disgust me, pain me, trouble me,
I do not abandon them, and I am afraid—
for I know their kind and their number.

North and east, south and west
the wheel of my life turns round and round
in constant inconstancy.

Of one thing alone am I confident:
You who have rent the heavens
and clothed yourself with flesh
will mercifully wash me clean through penance
and awaken me to life.

True Fear and Love

O Lord, it is out of fear
that you are called Lord,
and for the sake of love
you are called God;
and because you encompass all things with power
you are called almighty.

True and righteous are your judgments,
for a genuine fear of you destroys all fears,
and all loves unite
in true love of you.

Your power governs all powers.
I know that against you I can do nothing,
and I find my consolation in you.

Justice and Mercy

O Lord, I acknowledge your goodness:
I was not slain because of my sins;
instead, you left me my freedom.
In struggle with myself
I accomplish what is good,
but desire brings forth evil.

And yet you always judge justly
and never go beyond what is right.
In your power you protect and care for me with mercy.

Therefore I humble myself before you
and give glory to your name
for the sake of your loving-kindness.

Seeking God

I will fear you,
God my Lord;
who will help me
when I stand before you
and who will deliver me
from your terrifying judgment?
No one but you yourself,
the righteous God.
You I will seek
and always I will flee to you.

I will no longer let myself be influenced
by my twisted and selfish will.
I will turn back to you, my Father,
whom the devil refused to obey.

I will believe in you, my Lord,
the One in three persons,
you I will glorify and adore
and I will place my trust in you.

Forever I will carry your name in my heart.

The Soul's Lament in the Body

Oh, oh, you decaying ash,
why, oh why was I ever immersed in you
by my God,
so tangled in your needs
that when the devil whispers to me
I bring forth evil deeds as your accomplice?

Alas, I am not able
to hold back from sin!
I know that my deeds are unclean
before God and before all; why, then,
do I not fear you, my God,
you who judge all stain of sin
as the wicked work of Satan?

Oh, I forget you, my Creator,
for I did not turn aside as my reason bade
from the lusts of the flesh
out of fear and love for you!

Help me now, my God,
and through your blood
bring me up from the depths of my sin!
Draw me to you in your grace,
so that I may lift myself up to salvation.

Correction

With your scourge, O Lord of the world,
you have chastened me, a sinner,
and yet you did not surrender me
to the tortures of hell.

For in love I sought you,
confessed my sins to you.
I was patient and wise,
for I know that the verdict on my guilt
is righteous.

With the two wings
of the knowledge of good and evil
I will dare to fly to you
and to walk on the right way.

Insight

Nothing is sweeter to me, O my God,
than to hasten toward the Creator of the universe.
What I have vowed with heart and lips
I will accomplish, as I promised
before you, my righteous judge.

My deeds of trespass are past;
I will right myself according to your will,
avoid evil and do what is good.

Reason and insight burn within me,
they make their decision for true discipline;
for I would rather turn back
to the living God
than follow the devil
in foolish error.

In the Name of the Church

I am to be the bride of your Son
weak and fragile though I am.
Heavenly Father, I implore you:
do not hold back your help any longer!

Scattering and destruction threaten
the members of your beloved Son.
Defend me, defend us all;
turn your merciful eyes to us!

Oh, turn to us a little
so that we may not be utterly destroyed!

Lament

Oh, we are strangers!
What have we done?
We turned from the way and sinned.
We should have been daughters of the king,
but we have fallen
into the deep darkness of sin.

O bear us up, living sun,
on your shoulders,
to the heritage that belongs to us,
lost to us in Adam.

O King of Kings,
we are fighting your battle!

The Way and the Goal of Love

Teach me, O God, in the Holy Spirit
to walk in your ways,
to receive the food of life
that you give to the faithful
you elect and make holy.

Graciously receive me then
into the highest bliss;
let me rest in your arms.

From Virtue to Virtue

I followed you in faith, O Son of God,
on the traces of truth.
Through your humanity
you have saved all humanity.

O Guide of the Universe, lead me
to the fullness of all your gifts,
so that I, armed with your strength,
may go confidently on
from virtue to virtue.

If I thus set forth on the right path
and abandon myself,
I will taste the virtues,
drink and be strengthened by them.

The righteous one who thus loves God
will never be weary and surfeited,
but will live a life of blessing.

Contentment

I am enthroned above the stars
because I am content with your gifts.
I rejoice in the sweet notes of the drum
because I trust in you.

I kiss the sun, embrace the moon
and hold it fast; what you have made to spring up for me
is enough for me.
What more should I desire,
what things that I do not need?

Everything shows mercy to me.
In the house of my King I may dwell,
take my seat at the royal banquet,
for I am a daughter of the King.

Trust in Time of Trouble

Oh, unhappy mortal that I am,
once a living breath,
I am surrounded by the stench of sin;
I can no longer look joyfully to heaven.

Oh, oh, whence have I come,
and whither do I go?
What good to me is the goodness that God created
when I am going to hell?

Still will I trust in you, my God,
that through true penitence
I may be freed from the hellish tortures
I have deserved,
by your mercy.
Your grace consoles and strengthens me.

Remorse

Father, your child cries out to you,
for you want good things for it
and it knows you as God.

I drink from the dew of your blessing
and smile at you out of my remorseful heart.
Still in tears, I rejoice in you
and call out to you: God, come to my help!

With the sound of the harp the angels answer me,
they praise you when I call.
The dawn rays of your grace spread forth,
you give me the food of life
because I prayed to you for strength.

Eucharist

Who is this who gives me,
miserable, wretched person that I am,
yourself in the sweet sacrifice
as the Church's Bridegroom?
I call you brother
because you have become a man.
You drink from the divine mother's breast
mercy and truth,
the food of humanity.
The Divinity has become my mother,
for she formed me, awakened me,
and gave me life.
The Church's food is full of grace,
for you, the living bread
and source of living water,
provide her overflowing fullness
in the sacrament of your Body and Blood.
For the sake of my salvation
you became human.
You now make me a sharer
in your Body and Blood
so that no creature more may despise me,
since you for my sake
came into this world
and gave yourself up to me,
even though I rejected your commandments
and showed myself your enemy.

So let me kiss you, brother,
Son of God and Human One on earth.

Liberation

Lord God, in your merciful grace
wrench me, a sinner, from corruption,
so that I will not be hardened in denial of you.

Wrench me out of the lusts of the flesh,
that my body by the power of grace
may give forth the perfume of good works.

Wrench me, O God, out of my unclean deeds,
that the thorn of oblivion
may not nail me to corruption.

Let me with good conscience
and in the sweet odor of virtue
tread down filth
with the feet of my honest works.

My deserving is but a poor thing, O God;
treat me according to your loving-kindness!

Rescue

Lord, may your right hand lift me up,
cleansed by penitence, from my sins.
Strengthen my longing
to burn with the love of God;
I cannot get enough of it.

When I arise in penitence
I will not die in sin,
but rescued from death
I will live forever,
telling of your wondrous deeds
and fearing and loving you,
delivered from the corruption of death.

Fear of the Lord

Reverently I stand before you, O God.
I see my guilt as it is
and I do not turn away.

In love I sigh to you
and shrink before your judgment.
But I rejoice in your reward!
If I myself have not also deserved
to share in heavenly joys,
still I will keep myself free from guilt.

You give me to eat from the tree of life
because you find good works in me,
although the devil presses me hard.

You laid the foundation of holy works in me,
then pitched your tent with me.
So let me in turn dwell in your house!

Prayer of Faith

Faithfully I believe in you, O God,
and I accomplish works in faith.
Increase my joy in every virtue,
you, my joy, O Lord of the world!
In faith and love I will follow you,
for you are my Creator.

You give me what is good;
I lack nothing
that I ask and long for.
May faith teach me right petitions:
give me only what pleases you
and what lasts forever!

In great need I sigh to you
for myself or my brother, sister:
with holy and good works
let me achieve your love;
fulfill my righteous desires!

Under God's Protection

O God, you protect those who believe in you;
keep me safe in the shelter of your almighty power.
I take refuge under your wings,
in gratitude I honor and adore you.
I will never look up to a God
who deceives me and does not know me.

But deliver me from the rebellion
of the evil, torturing spirits
in the lust of my flesh,
and give me perfect victory!
Let my soul rejoice in my body
because the body brings forth the soul's eternal reward.

Prayer for Healing

Oh, whence have I come
and what am I doing now?
With a loud lament I groan
because I have mingled my knowledge of you, O God,
with the filth of sin.

Have mercy on me, O Lord,
I have soiled my soul with sin!
Heal the weals of my wounds
for it is against you that I have sinned.

Teach me more and more, my God,
to do holy and good deeds
so that my utterly unsettled soul
may receive healing from you.

Longing

My home is in heaven;
there I meet creatures as well.
God's love is my lust,
I will build the tower of longing.

What you will, O God, that I will do.
With the wings of good will
I fly above the brow of heaven
to do your will.

Nothing remains for me to seek or to want,
I long only for what is holy.

O God, let me be the harpstrings
and guitar music of your love!

Visitation

My God, I call to you
in bitter repentance, with wounded heart:
Heal me, kind Father;
visit me in your mercy,
for you alone are my God.

Guided by your grace
I behold you in your works.
It is you whom I seek in the simplicity of my heart,
and in my weeping I cry out for you.

You dwell in the power of my soul;
my body must do penance for my sins.
The eye of repentance sees
the futility of my evil deeds.
But now, receive me!

In the Power of God

O my God, without your help
I, unworthy human that I am,
cannot hold to my decision
to live a virgin life before you.
Conceived and born in sin,
out of my own strength
I cannot conquer the lusts of the flesh.

Give me, then, the fiery gift
to quench this burning in your power,
so that with a right desire
I may drink from the source of life
that gives me joy.

Truly I am nothing but crumbling ashes;
I behold the works of darkness
and not of light.

In the Holy Spirit

O God most high,
in your honor
I make my vows to you,
for without you I can do nothing;
I am left to my own devices.

Only the grace of the Holy Spirit
that you kindle in me
can enable me.

Healing Wounds

Why am I so deeply troubled
and confused in my soul,
when through the grace of God
I could banish the wounds of sin
with sighing and tears?

Through your wounds, my Lord,
the nails and the lance
that you endured for my sins,
I hope for redemption.

Redemption

Redeemed by the blood of the Lamb of God,
let us rejoice with all our hearts
and be glad with all our souls in you,
triune God, who sustain us.
We will remember the heavenly reward
for all the sufferings and dangers
that the enemies of truth have prepared for us.
They are nothing to us
compared to the joy
with which we taste of your commandments.
Whoever does the works of sanctity
receives you in true and perfect love;
you give all good things to those who love,
and your last gift to them
is eternal life.

Touched by God

What is wrong with me?
I know nothing that is good;
I cannot even think of it.

I, a sinner—alas, what can I do?
I do not know and cannot even think
what will now become of me
because of my many, many sins.

Oh, where shall I turn,
to whom shall I run for help
to cover my shameful sins
and remove them with repentance?

I will turn back in my heart,
return in true repentance
to you, God, who have touched my wounds.

Awakened from the sleep of death,
I will not sin again
in thought, word, or deed.

Redemptive Penitence

Why was I born
to such great misdeeds?
In my soul I have sinned
against you, my God.

I sigh to you
who deigned to take on Adam's shape
from the virgin.

I firmly trust
that you do not despise me,
but free me from my sins.

In the countenance of your sacred humanity
receive me in grace,
for I repent with all my heart.

Life After Death

A happy life is what I desire
in the peace of eternity.
Even in the time of my life's blooming,
as I grow and ripen toward holiness,
I will remember my Creator
with good and holy deeds.

The time will come when flesh and blood
will shrink, down to the bones.
The ashes of the body will sink
into the dust of the earth from which I was made;
they will then be absorbed in another life.

The spirit that animated my body
will leave it and return
to the Lord of creation,
who graciously bestowed it on my body.

You, Creator, are like a blacksmith
who kindles the fire with a bellows,
turns the iron around and around
to finish the work at hand.

When, guided by good deeds,
I find my way home to eternal joy
let me see the purest light.
Let me hear the songs of the angels
and retrieve in joy
the longed-for garment of my body
that I have put aside.

Victorious in God

My Creator and Lord, you are my strength,
without you I can do nothing that is good,
for it is through your Spirit that I live.
It is that Spirit that sets me in motion
and shows me the way I should go.

I will call to you, God and Lord;
let me walk in the way of your commandments
as the deer rushes to the springs.

Lead me out, over earthly desires
to the heights of strength and victory.
When I attain to heavenly bliss
I will never tire of singing your praise.

Love

Teach me
with the breath of the Holy Spirit
so that pure water
may flow from me,
that tears may flow
from sighing after good deeds,
and a sweet smell pour forth
from holy works.
In the day I will exercise
the virtue of serenity,
and by night I will salve
all pains.

Bliss

I call to you, O my God,
and you answer me.
I plead and your kindness
gives me what I desire;
with you I find what I seek.

Filled with awe and joy
I strike the harp before you, my God,
for I turn all my works toward you.
All my hope I place in you
and I rest content in your arms.

Plea for Forgiveness

You, to whose power all things are subject,
see the blood that was shed
for all humanity,
and forgive us our sins.

We are the children of trespass
and we should have paid for it.
In the wickedness of our hearts
we have not done so.
We did not keep our baptismal promise;
we transgressed your commandments
and threw away our innocence.

But you are kind; do not punish us
according to our great evil,
but in your love forgive us
our transgression,
for out of love,
in reverence for our Redeemer,
we have with all our hearts forgiven
the evil that others have done to us.

Now be gracious to us, O God,
because you are just and good!

Hope

O kindest Father, spare sinners!
You did not forsake the exiles,
but carried them on your shoulders.
We, too, will not perish,
for we place our hope in you.

Exaltation

Let us praise the Lord, our God,
who has exalted us
because we have conquered in God's name.

Our strength is God's honor,
for we have triumphed
over God's enemies and our own
because we are faithful
and believe steadfastly in God.

Heavenly Joy

When I open my eyes,
my God, on all that you have created
I have heaven already in my hands.

Serenely I gather in my lap
roses and lilies and all green things
while I praise your works.

My own works I ascribe entirely to you.
Gladness springs forth from sorrow,
and joy brings happiness.

Sanctity

I call to you, O God:
give me what I need to live!
You have good plans for me;
I may see you and know you.

My good conscience senses you, my God;
I strike the harp of prayer
when in adoration I behold you.
Girded with continence,
I bloom in blissful joy.

Perfect, O God, your works
through the armed band of Christ the King
that I lead forth to battle.

True Faith

Admonished by the Holy Spirit
and with an upright mind
we will approach the highest bliss,
begin what is good with peaceful hearts
and complete it in piety.

May sisterly and brotherly love be kindled in peace,
imitate your goodness, O God,
and behold the needs of humanity.
So may our hearts' true faith
be perfected in simplicity and purity.

Praise and Petition

Praise to you, O Christ, King of the angels!
Who are you, O God,
who bore in your heart
this great decision,
who foiled the devil's cunning
in the toll collectors and sinners
who now shine in the goodness of the Father?

Therefore praise to you, O King!

O you almighty Father!
From you flows a stream with a fiery glow.
Draw your children across the water
with a favorable wind in their sails
to the heavenly city, Jerusalem!

Songs

The Saving Name

O almighty Father,
we are in great need,
so we implore you,
implore you through your Word,
through that which you bestow on us in all plenitude,
what we need to live.
Look now, Father,
according to your name,
look on us and help us,
so that we may not perish utterly
and your name will not be obscured in us.
Deign to come to our aid
through this, your holy name!

Creator and Redeemer

O ancient power of eternity,
in your heart
you ordered the universe.
Through your Word you created all things
as you desired.
And this, your Word, took on flesh
in the form derived from Adam.
Thus from his garment was removed
the heavy curse.

How great is your kindness, O Savior!
Through your incarnation
you have liberated all things.
Of the breath of God you became human
without the bonds of sin.

Glory to you, Father, and to your Son
with the Holy Spirit.

Thus from his garment was removed
the heavy curse.

The Good Shepherd

O shepherd of souls,
O first of Words
through which we all were created,
may it please you, may it please:
free us from our fear
and fragility.

Destined for Salvation

O eternal God,
through the glowing embers of your love
make us members
wrought with the same love
with which you begot your own Son
in the first red dawn
of your creation.

Look on the trouble that came upon us;
free us for the sake of your Son
and bring us to the joy of salvation.

Father and Son

O glorious Father!
With glowing haste we hurry to you,
we sigh for you with the loving penitence
that we have received from you.

O Christ, so glorious and altogether beautiful,
you are the resurrection to life.
Help us to remain steadfast
and to rejoice with you.
Never let us be separated from you!

The Blood of Christ

O bloody deed that cried to heaven
when all the elements broke forth
in uproar, shouting for dismay
because the blood of the Creator had touched them:

Oh, soothe our affliction!

Sanctification

O fire of the consoling Spirit,
Life of the life of all created things!

Holy are you:
you give life to every form.
Holy are you:
you cleanse festering wounds.
Holy are you:
you salve the fearfully injured.
Breath of all sanctity, fire of love,
sweet tasting at our breast,
The pleasant scent of virtues
you sink into our hearts.

Purest spring in which we see
how God gathers the strays
and seeks the lost.

O protector of life,
you hope of the members for unity,
O girdle of moral honor,
heal the saints!

Shelter those whom the enemy holds captive,
free those who lie in chains;
the power of God will save them.

You powerful way that traverses all things,
heights and depths of earth,
you ordain and encompass all in one.

Through you the clouds waft
and the breezes blow,
stones drip
and brooks burst forth from their springs,
making green things sprout from the earth.

At all times you bring forth people
full of understanding,
made glad by the breath of Wisdom.

Therefore be praise to you,
Voice of praise,
Joy of life,
Hope and powerful glory,
because you give the gifts of light.

The Spirit Who Gives Life

Holy Spirit,
life-giving Life,
Dynamo of the universe and root of creation,
cleanse your creation of its filth,
drive out sin and oil its wounds.

O glowing Life, worthy of praise,
awaken and reawaken the universe!

In the Fire of the Spirit

O Spirit of Fire, praise to you!
Human hearts glow from your heat;
the tents of souls
gather their strength.
The will ascends
and fills the soul with desire,
longing,
burns it like a torch.

But you always wield the sword
and cut off
what poisonous fruit
brings forth through malicious murder
when fog shrouds the will and its desires.

The spirit disciplines will and desire.
But when the spirit stretches itself upward
and longs to look the Evil One in the eye,
to stare wickedness in the face,
you swiftly burn it with fire
as you will.

When reason bows down to the depths
through evil deeds,
you hold it in check if you will,
and you break it and lead it back
through the power of your proving.

If evil draws its sword against you,
you turn it back into its own heart
as you did with the first fallen angel

when you cast the tower of his pride
down to hell.

You built another tower
out of toll collectors and sinners,
so that they would confess
their sins and deeds before you.

Therefore all creatures praise you:
they live from you,
for you are the most precious ointment
for broken limbs
and festering wounds,
which you transform into precious pearls.

Now gather us all to you in grace
and lead us on the right path.

Amen.

Triune Life

Praise to you, O Trinity,
You are accord and life.

The bands of angels praise you,
you wondrous, secret light;
hidden from human sight
you are in all things life.

Praise of Wisdom

O power of Wisdom,
you drew your circles,
encompassed the universe
on the one road
that leads to life.

You have three powers
like three wings:
The one carries you to the heights;
the second lifts itself from the earth;
but the third beats everywhere.

O Wisdom, to you all praise is due!

Mary, the New Creation

O glittering gem! The sun's purest ornament
poured forth as a bubbling spring of life
in you, out of the heart of the Father.
Through this, his sole Word,
he created the primeval element of the earth
that Eve spoiled.

In you the Father formed that Word
into a human being;
therefore you are the glowing primal matter
through which the Word
sent forth the powers of all virtues with a breath,
as it awakened the form of every creature
to life.

Election

O lovely sprout full of greening power
from the stem of Jesse,
what a great event is this:
As the eagle lifts its eyes
to the sun,
so the divine glance
fell on the most beautiful of women
when the Father from heaven,
O Virgin,
looked into your purity
and his Word became
flesh in you.

Your virginal heart was enlightened
in mystical ways by God's mystery
and wondrous bloomed from you,
O Virgin, a bright flower.

Praise be to God the Father,
the Son, and the Holy Spirit!

Mother of God

Hail to you, Mary,
source of life;
you rebuilt salvation,
overcame death,
trod upon the serpent
toward whom Eve,
swollen with pride,
turned with uplifted head.

You trod it down,
for you bore the Son of God
breathed into you by the Holy Spirit.
Hail to you, sweet and lovely Mother!
You bore for the world your Son,
sent from heaven,
breathed into you by God's Holy Spirit.

Mediatrix

O glorious mother of sacred healing power,
through your holy Son
you poured oil into the harsh wounds of death
that Eve opened, to the torture of souls.

You have destroyed death
and built up life;
pray for us to your Son,
Mary, Star of the Sea!

O life-giving mediatrix,
festive adornment
and most precious of all joys
that in you never come to their end!

Pray for us, Mary!

To Mary

Hail, greening twig full of life's power!
In the pangs of the Spirit and the seeking of holy men
you came to light.
The time came when your branches bloomed.
Hail to you, hail!

The sun's rays shone like the scent of balsam from you,
for in you bloomed the beautiful flower
that scented the wilted herbs
so that they all sprang forth in full green life.

Heaven dropped dew on the grass,
the whole earth was fruitful,
and grain brought forth its yield.
The birds of the air nested in it.

So there was food for the people
and great was the joy of table companions.

Therefore you are not lacking in joy
O mild virgin.
Eve despised it all.

But now let the Most High be praised!

Praise of Mary

Hail to you, O Virgin!
You overflow with glory,
you pure creation.

Hail to you, chastity's darling,
foundation of all sanctity,
God's pleasure.

For the power of the Most High
flowed into you
because the Word of God
in you put on
the garment of flesh.

Gleaming white are you
like a lily,
because God beheld your face
before any other creature.

O beauty, love's incomparable delight,
God was so enraptured with you
as to place deep within you
fire, heat, and tender love.

So the Son fed from you.
Then your body sprang with joy
as the symphony of heaven
sounded forth from you,
because you, O Virgin,
bore the Son of the Father.

Your chastity
is glory
in God.

Your womb rejoiced
like the grass
on which the dew rests,
lending its fresh and greening power.

So it was in you,
O Mother of all joy.

Now may the dawn arise,
joy for the whole Church.
And may a symphony break forth
in praise of you, O Virgin, Mother of God—
full of love.

Mary, Our Hope

O greening twig,
in your nobility you stand
and rise up
like the dawn.

Rejoice now, and be glad!
Free us weak humans
from our bad habits
and stretch forth your hand
to lift us from the earth.

Virgin Mother of God

O twig, diadem for the royal purple,
you rest, enclosed as in a fortress.
You grow green and bloom so differently
from Adam, the father of the human race.

Hail to you, hail!
New life sprang from your womb
because Adam stole life from his children.

O flower, neither dew nor raindrops
caused you to sprout;
the wind did not blow upon you,
but the divine glory
begot you on the noblest bough.

O branch, God saw your blossom
on the first day of creation.
From his word, O praiseworthy Virgin,
he created the golden primal element.

How powerful the side of the man!
From it God created the figure of the woman
as a mirror of divine beauty
to embrace the whole creation.

Therefore the heavenly harps sound
and the whole earth stands astonished
at how much God loved you—
praise to you, O Mary!

Oh, how we must lament and sorrow
that such a sad offense

came upon the woman through the serpent's cunning!
Made by God to be mother of all,
she wounded her heart with the wound of ignorance
and brought great suffering on her offspring.

But from your womb, O Dayspring,
came forth the new sun
who rooted out the sin of Eve
and brought forth more blessing through you
than Eve cost humanity.

Therefore, O Saving Woman, bearing
new light for the human race,
gather the members of your Son
into the heavenly harmony!

Mary the Prophet

When we, unhappy mortals,
shamed from generation to generation,
are waylaid on the pilgrim path,
you call to us with a prophetic voice
and lift us up from our hard fall.

Praise to you, O Mary!

In the Light of the Angel Choirs

O glorious angels, living light!
In the dark mystery of every creature
you, before the throne of God,
see with burning desire the eye of God;
you can never be sated with it.
What glorious joy is contained in your nature,
which remained untouched by any evil deed
as it once arose in your companion,
the angel who fell.
He wanted to fly above the towers
hidden in the heart of God;
tortuously twisted he sank in ruins.
The creations of the divine fingers
he, with his cunning counsel, made the tools of his trap.

But you, O angels, protectors of the nations,
whose nature is reflected in your faces,
O archangels, who receive righteous souls,
you Powers, Dominions, and Principalities,
Virtues and Thrones,
united in the mystery of the Five,
O Cherubim, Seraphim,
Seals on the mysteries of God,
praise to you! You behold the dark chamber
of the eternal heart at its source;
for you see, face to face,
the heart of the Father
as it breathes forth its inner power.

Wedding

O virgin Church, how great your pain
that at the cunning counsel of the serpent
the wild wolf tore your beloved children
from your side.

But how precious is the Savior's blood,
who beneath the victorious banner of the cross
wed himself to the Church
and won back her children!

Mother Church

Rejoice now in the depths of your heart,
O mother Church, for your children
are gathered in holy unanimity
in your arms.

But you, O wicked serpent,
are thwarted, for your prey
that you thought to have devoured
shines forth in the blood of the son of God.

Therefore praise to you, O King Most High:
Alleluia!

Prevenient Grace

O joy beyond joy,
that you, my God, do these things:
you give your grace to those who have no thought of you.
A chick does not understand the flight of the adult bird,
but even to the chick you have given wings.

You take pleasure in those
who do not even know themselves;
for their voices call to you:
O God, my God who created me,
all my works are yours!

Let the whole Church rejoice!

Song of the Virgins

O tender lover who surrounds us,
preserve us in our virginity!
Alas for us, we came forth
from dust and Adam's fall!
It is hard for us to resist
the sweetness of the apple.
Raise us up, O Savior Christ!

We deeply long to follow you,
but it is not easy for us, miserable beings
rightly to imitate you, the King of the angels,
spotless and without sin.

Still we trust in you:
you will seek gems in the dust.
We appeal to you as our Bridegroom, Consoler,
and Savior on the cross.

Bound to you in bridal bonds, in your blood,
we seek you alone, O Son of God,
as our husband.
O Most Beautiful, full of joy and most precious odor,
we sigh constantly for you
in our miserable exile.

When will we see you in this world
where you dwell in our souls?
In our hearts we embrace you
as if you were present.

You, strong lion, tore open the heavens
and came down into the womb of the virgin.

As victor over death you brought
life to the golden city;
now let us dwell there!—and abide
in you, beloved Bridegroom.
You have rescued us from the vengeance of the devil
who led astray our first parents.

The Golden City

Jerusalem, you golden city
adorned with royal purple!
O edifice of the Father's goodness,
Light that never darkens,
you glow in the morning rays
and in the heat of the sun.

Your windows, Jerusalem,
are wonderfully adorned with topaz and sapphire.
Jerusalem, your foundations
have been built of rejected stones—
toll collectors and sinners
who once were lost sheep.
But then, found by the Son of God,
they hastened to you and were put in place.

So your walls sparkle with living stones
that, in the great zeal of good will,
flew there like the clouds of heaven.
Like red gold, O Jerusalem,
your towers shimmer and sparkle
with the red and white of the saints
and God's great glory
that fills you, Jerusalem.

O you bejeweled and crowned
inhabitants of Jerusalem,
hasten to help us, the servants of God!
We are laboring in exile.

Prayer of Christ

In the beginning all creation was greening,
the flowers were blooming in the middle of time;
when the power of life dried up.

Then, Father, you looked at me
and saw yourself reflected!
My body is attacked by exhaustion,
my little ones fall victim
to human weakness.
Remember, O Father! The hopes of the beginning
should not have withered;
the golden number is not yet full!

It was not then your intention
ever to turn away your eyes
until you saw my body
adorned with jewels.

For the sake of my derided members
I fall in exhaustion.
Look, Father,
let me show you my wounds!

It hurts me that my members
turn from me and listen
to the Son of Perdition.
Nevertheless I will bring home again
those among them who have fallen.

Father, look, I am your Son!
Look with love on me,

the love with which you sent me into the world.
Behold the wounds
through which, as you commanded,
I redeemed the human race.
Have mercy on them, and do not let
their names be erased
from the book of life!

Through the blood of my wounds
bring them in penitence
back to you.

All you people, bend the knee
before your Father
that he may extend to you
his helping hand!